A GUIDED JOURNAL FOR
ADAPTING TO LIFE
OVERSEAS

Finding Home Abroad

Trisha Carter
Rachel Yates

"A **must-have** personal resource for first-time international assignees and their accompanying partners, a great complementary tool for any cross-cultural trainer or coach, and an invaluable resource for expats no matter how seasoned they may be. Gentle guidance from experts through the relocation adjustment cycle, tips to help you deal with expat stress and keep a track of self-learnings."

Anne-Claude Lambelet
Intercultural Competence & Career Development Coach
Director FIGT.org, Chair FIGT Switzerland,
www.aclambelet-consulting.com

"The research is conclusive: When expats take the time to write down reflections in the midst of new cross-cultural experiences, it's proven to enhance their cultural intelligence (CQ). But many don't know where to begin. Now there's no excuse! Trisha Carter and Rachel Yates have put together an excellent resource to help sojourners record their intercultural reflections. Rooted in research but written for practitioners, *Finding Home Abroad* will be a huge help to those who use it, as well as to their families and organizations."

David A Livermore, author and thought leader
in CQ and global leadership
Best-selling author, *Cultural Intelligence:
Improving Your CQ to Engage Our
Multicultural World* and *Leading With Cultural
Intelligence: The New Secret to Success*
http://www.culturalq.com

"*Finding Home Abroad* is a common-sense guide to recording your thoughts, reactions and emotions as you journey through a foreign landscape. It encourages you to get to know your new location from the inside out, leaving assumptions behind. This guide is a gem – don't leave home without it!"

Apple Gidley
Author, *Expat Life Slice by Slice*
www.applegidley.com

"Timeless classic advice can be yours with *Finding Home Abroad*. I really liked this book – it's bursting with easy to follow instructions, practical tips and advice on how to get started in mapping out and writing a log of your new journey and emotions, and offers an opportunity to learn and review along the way. A great read for anyone about to embark on a new international work opportunity."

Ruth Lockwood
Group Director, Relocation Services, Santa Fe
www.santaferelo.com/global-network/corporate-office/

"This guided journal is a 'must have' for any prospective expat – an excellent reflection and development tool to put you firmly in control of the relocation process from the outset, providing a productive, proactive and creative framework to help develop your global mindset."

Wendy Wilson
Executive coach and global mobility researcher
www.wendywilsonconsulting.com

First Edition 2014

First Published in the United Kingdom by Summertime Publishing

© Copyright Trisha Carter and Rachel Yates

All rights reserved. No part of this publication may be reproduced, stored in or introduced into a retrieval system, or transmitted, in any form, or by any means (electronic, mechanical, photocopying recording or otherwise) without the prior written permission of the publisher.

This book is sold subject to the condition that it shall not, by way of trade or otherwise, be lent, resold, hired out, or otherwise circulated without the publisher's prior consent in any form of binding or cover other than that in which it is published and without a similar condition including this condition being imposed on the subsequent purchaser.

ISBN 978-1-909193-67-3

Design by www.creationbooth.com

May your travels broaden your mind, deepen your knowledge, widen your friendships and strengthen your skills.

Contents

Introduction...II

How To Use This Journal.. IV

Preparing To Launch 1

Just Landed!..35

Checking In...61

One Month In...89

Three Month Milestone... 113

Appendices

1. The Gaining Clarity Exercise 125
2. Get The Knowledge...127
3. Moving Countdown Checklist 133
4. Developing your Cultural Intelligence (CQ) 139
5. Essential Documents...141
6. 'In Case Of Emergency' Plan 145
7. But Wait There's More 149

About The Authors 151

Introduction

An international move!

Congratulations – you are embarking on a journey that will be exciting, enriching but often uncomfortable. Whenever we go through changes, whether personal, professional or geographical, we are faced with many challenges, within our environments and also within ourselves.

These challenges have the power to be positive and negative, but there are numerous strategies to help you transition well. Many of them are contained within this journal, which has been designed to support your success.

It will help you document and explore your experiences – the landscapes, cultures, relationships and your own personal transition. It will help you look through more observant eyes to remember, reflect and shape your responses.

We wrote this book with you in mind. We know from personal experience how different and how difficult moving across cultures can be, and we want to provide you with a way of not only recording the highs and lows of the transition, but also of using them to improve your own cross-cultural skills.

Together we have over 40 years of international experience, both as expats, accompanying partners and within our professional fields. Trisha is an expat, organisational psychologist, intercultural trainer and CQ specialist. Rachel is an expat, author, lecturer and speaker. We have both experienced the challenges that crossing cultures brings, a journey echoed by the research, our training and coaching clients, and the expats who respond to our blogs and newsletters.

These stories led to the development of this journal. Research has long acknowledged the difficulty of adapting to a new location, and the crucial role cultural intelligence plays in the adaptation process. Journaling, whether as part of a cross-cultural program or as a personal reflection tool, can help build cultural intelligence skills and provide a place to observe, reflect, process and ultimately give you the ability to adapt well.

It's a wonderful tool for combating the sense of powerlessness and loss of control, which can accompany a huge life change. It helps to focus on your vision for your new life, encourages you to acknowledge the world around you, to take note, and to question your reactions.

Journaling offers an outlet for expressing emotions and then allows you to recognise you are not controlled or defined by those emotions – they are simply your feelings at a particular point in time. Seeing your thoughts and responses in writing helps keep things in perspective, to reflect and even laugh at yourself, or the situations you find yourself in.

Your journal provides an important barometer of your progress in adapting to the new location. As you review previous entries you begin to recognise your own growth and development and can celebrate your victories, however small – your growing confidence in navigating neighbourhoods, speaking the language or finding new friends.

This is no ordinary travel journal. It is carefully structured to support you in building your skills, adapting to the new culture and developing the resilience to flourish in your new home. It features prompts designed to stimulate your thinking and help you to observe more closely both your new environment and your responses to that environment.

Right now, you may be feeling overwhelmed with the tasks at hand – packing, paperwork and the many details of an international move. Don't worry – we have included a set of checklists at the back of the book to help you keep track of the moving process, leaving you a little freer to focus on your personal journey

Further resources are available at our website www.expatjournals.com. See the appendices at the back of the book for more details.

How To Use This Journal

Embracing the process of recording your thoughts, feelings and actions regularly allows you unique insight into your own journey across cultures.

Try to write whenever you have strong feelings, catching the story as it happens. In the words of Dr. James W. Pennebaker, a pioneer in the use of journaling as a development tool:

'In your writing, I'd like you to really let go and explore your ... emotions and thoughts. ... Don't worry about spelling, grammar, or sentence structure.'

Commit to writing, but in the way that suits you best. There are no rules to this journal – you use it whenever you want to write. It may be a single word, a simple sentence, or pages of thoughts, feelings or observations. Simply write what you need to write.

The prompts at the heading of each page are designed to help you observe both the world around you and your responses to it. Follow the prompts where they speak to you and your current situation, but don't be limited by them.
We have put the framework for your journey in place, it's now up to you to let it take you wherever you need to go.

Preparing To Launch

This first part of your journal can be used to explore your needs, expectations, priorities and hopes for your new life. If you need a little more help, we have included an exercise in the appendix to help guide you through the process. As your thoughts develop, make note of them in your journal, but don't expect to get it all on paper first time – this is a part you might want to revisit regularly, because as your familiarity with your location changes, so might your expectations.

What Matters To You?

What are your plans and dreams for this new stage of your life?

What you are hoping to be a part of, to see, to experience?

Our goals, plans and dreams motivate and energise us.

What things do you think you will like about this place, this culture, this country?

What are you excited about?

Travel can broaden your mind if you are open and curious.

What will be different?

Differences can be fascinating. Enjoy them.

What worries or frightens you?

What do you already know and what do you need to find out?

This is a great place for you to brainstorm all the gaps in your knowledge, and start making a list of potential sources of information. Don't limit yourself to books and travel guides – consider using government websites, social media, expat networks for example. If you don't know where to start, head over to the appendix for a list of suggested resources for general information.

Finding out more about any location gives rise to a huge range of emotions. Some of the information will cause anxiety, some will spark excitement. Putting strategies in place to address those feelings as you experience them is vital to your emotional well-being. What are you doing to help manage the stresses of transition? What are the things you find relaxing and refreshing?

Between now and your departure, chances are there will be two main themes dominating your days – the physical move and the emotional process of saying goodbye. We have included checklists in the appendix to remind you of some of the essential tasks you need to get done, but don't ignore your emotional well-being. Use the next few pages to note down and reflect on how you are feeling as you start the process of leaving.

Lists can help capture the important things your brain struggles to remember and free your brain to be more creative or to relax when you need to. Journals can be about lists and notes-to-self as well as the deeper observations.

Few of us look forward to saying goodbye, especially to those people who have become important in our lives. Take time to acknowledge the role each has played in shaping who you are and how they have enriched your life.

As you say goodbye to family, friends and special places take a moment to be thankful for all you have had here to make your life meaningful.

Just Landed!

Welcome! You've arrived! You are now in a new environment but what are your first impressions? What immediately strikes you?

What interesting things happen as you arrive and travel to your accommodation?

Often it is the environment around us which we notice first – the infrastructure, the buildings, the facilities. Or possibly the natural environment – the weather, the scenery, the birds, animals and plants.

Breathe, observe, stay open.

Increase your observation skills by becoming very aware of what you see and hear around you. No two places are the same, even if the differences are subtle, take note. Tune in to what you see, what you hear, or what you smell!

Look for the shared and delight in the different.

People's behaviour is often fascinating – both the similarities and differences. How do they initially appear – happy, busy, friendly – or more distant than you are accustomed to?

Small things, such as what side of the footpath or sidewalk people walk on, can make a big difference to your sense of fitting in when you observe and adapt your behaviour to mirror the locals.

How do people behave on public transport? In cafes? Do they queue up and wait to be served or call out orders from the crowd?

It's not right or wrong – it's just different.

Consider the conversations going on around you as you sit in a café or on public transport. How do strangers talk to each other? How do service personnel, such as waiters and shop assistants, talk with their customers? And how do locals respond to those conversations?

What is the level of volume in a conversation? Does it differ when people are inside compared to when they are outside?

What sort of food and drink do the locals enjoy? How does this compare to the food and drink you usually enjoy? Are you experimenting with things that are a little different for you?

Look for the shared and delight in the different.

When you meet new people at work or local service providers, how do they greet and interact with you? Is it a more formal or less formal environment than you are accustomed to? What things are you noticing about people generally?

People are people, no matter where in the world they come from, or where you find them.

What might you be doing that is seen as different or strange? What reactions have you had, and do you know what those responses really mean?

Remember the locals may not value what I consider important and I may not value what is precious to them.

Who are the specific individuals you have met and what are your thoughts about them?

Think of the individual variation within your own country and culture and remember that your new location may be similarly diverse.

As you start to explore your new location, you might compare and contrast both your home and your host cultures – and perhaps others you have experienced. There may be both positive and negative comparisons. Do you notice a pattern in your observations?

Have you found places selling the foods or drinks that were favourites for you back home? It can be great to discover a familiar treat in an unexpected place. Keep an eye out for surprises!

Checking In

It's time to 'check in' with your feelings – how you are responding to the differences around you? Your responses and how you manage them are crucial to your ability to thrive in a new culture. When you are struggling, remind yourself that you are not controlled or defined by your feelings – know they will pass and more positive ones will emerge.

Breathe, observe, stay open.

Write about the situation which triggered the negative feelings, and then put your journal down and go and do something that gives you joy – reading a book, watching a movie, or whatever makes you feel good.

Tough times are part of life. They will pass, and you will be stronger.

What are you observing at work or in the neighbourhoods around you? How are buildings and offices different from those you are familiar with? How do people dress for their different roles – work, family time, errands, nights out?

Think how boring an aquarium would be if all the fish were the same.

How do people spend their leisure time? Why?

What are you doing in your leisure time? Why?

Sharing is the swiftest way to build relationships. A smile, a meal, a journey, an experience.

When you are in meetings or observing others talking together, note the 'turn-taking' behaviour in conversations. Are people comfortable speaking over the top of each other or are there pauses between each speaker? How do these patterns compare to your natural pattern of speech? Will you need to speed up and leap in – or slow down and 'hold your tongue'?

It's not right or wrong – it's just different.

Do people seem religious? Are there many signs of spiritual belief and behaviour? If you have your own beliefs, how will you demonstrate them? Are there others to share your celebrations? How are things similar or different in your spiritual tradition here?

Recognise that everyone is unique, and will reflect their culture, background, experience in a way that is individual to them. Don't make assumptions.

How is work or everyday life progressing?

The local media can give you great insight into the world around you. What are the newspapers and television channels, and are there differences between them? Are there any available in your language? What does the tone and content say about local values and interests?

In these early days, you often view the location and culture as an outsider, as if on a vacation. Embrace it and explore – take the time to soak in the sights, sounds, history and culture from a more relaxed perspective.

One of the most helpful sources of information can be a 'cultural mentor'. Your organization may provide you with a cross-cultural coach or a mentor at work, or you may find someone who can take that role for you. Take note of things you find confusing, and use them as a basis for your discussions.

You have made it through the first few weeks! Already some things will be familiar to you – this means the adaptation process is well underway. Recognize how quickly you have built familiarity and routine in your new location and congratulate yourself and your family members!

Is the local language easy for you to understand? If you are familiar with the language how are you finding the local accent or slang? What interesting expressions have you heard? If you are learning a new language, keep listening to those around you and take every opportunity to practice.

Think about why you wanted to travel. If all you wanted was the comfort of home, you would never have started this journey.

Our culture shapes the way we use language and conversation. Casual conversation is not as easy as it seems – what differences have you observed in communication around you? Volume, tone, pace and phrasing all vary hugely across cultures.

Listen to your gut reaction but don't let it control you. Remember it's not right or wrong – it's just different.

If you have moved with family how are they adapting? What things are they finding exciting and what things are they struggling with? If you have left family members at home, how are you keeping in touch?

Many people who move find it helpful to set a 'date' for communicating and regularly calling to talk. It's a great way to recognise the importance of your relationship and the need to keep connected.

One Month In

Sometimes people reach the four to six week milestone and experience a 'low' period. Often it's a feeling that the 'honeymoon' period is over and the realities of real life, away from your support networks, is setting in. The down days are just you acknowledging the loss, the struggle and the uncertainty which comes with every transition, so listen when they happen. Write about the time and emotions before and during these periods, and reflect on what may trigger them, and what helps to put you back on track.

Take time to do some of the fun things you had in mind when you first decided to move – whether exploring the local sights, sitting on a beach, reading a book in the garden or simply watching the sun set.

*Remind yourself of the reasons you moved here
and the good times you have had so far.*

Music can be a great way to change your mood. What music uplifts you, resonates with you or makes you sing out loud?

What music do the locals enjoy? Have you listened to live music or a concert? What music do your friends enjoy?

Look for the shared and delight in the different.

What did you do for exercise in your home country? Are there similar opportunities in your new location? What do the locals do for exercise – is there something new you would like to try?

Have you explored outside of your city or town? Visit the surrounding areas. Enjoy the different scenery and location.

Don't underestimate how much learning is involved in any transition – not only learning a language or a new job role, but also how to navigate your surroundings, how to communicate, to behave and even to support your family members. Everything which was second nature before your move has been revisited, and it has an impact on your mental and physical health. Schedule time and resources to rest and regroup regularly, but also take time to record what you have learned, starting from the first moment you stepped off the plane. What could you now teach your former self?

Hold your former self gently. How much kinder would you be to someone else than you were to yourself? It's only in hindsight we realise the enormity of what we have accomplished, so try to be gentle with yourself as you go through the journey.

Think about the friendships you are beginning to build with the people around you. Who are the people that are becoming part of your community – locals, work colleagues, other expats? How did your relationship begin?

People are people, no matter where in the world they come from or where you find them.

You have spent some time in your new workplace by now. What are the differences and similarities you are observing? Are things done differently in the new workplace and how are you coping with these changes?

Remember the locals may not value what I consider important and I may not value what is precious to them.

You may have come across situations where you are uncomfortable with the way someone has spoken to you. Bear in mind it might be a cultural difference in the way of communicating rather than an expression of anger or disapproval towards you. Be patient, know that you are still learning, and reflect on your own communication to make sure your meaning is clear. Ask a cultural mentor or coach for help and guidance.

Remember to laugh at yourself – laughter is the best medicine.

Remember to celebrate your anniversaries and achievements. You have been here a couple of months. You have found your way around your locality and your workplace. You have met many new people and worked hard. Read over what you have written so far, and take time to celebrate how far you have come, both geographically and culturally.

Apart from the locals, you have probably come across other cultural groups. Have you found any you are especially comfortable with? What are the characteristics you share?

Find your support team – whoever they might be – and use them well.

How is your search for a new social circle going? Look at all avenues, such as joining a club or interacting with as many people from work as possible. You may find some circles are easier to break into than others; spend some time considering why this might be – is it something within you, or within the group?

Remember it takes time and shared experiences to make friends.

In your everyday life and work you are now constantly faced with a choice – acting like a local or acting as you would back home. Try to make those choices conscious – review how you act each time and how effective each approach was. Switching behaviours builds flexibility and adaptability.

A helpful question when you get stuck and things aren't getting done: "What would you suggest I do?"

Three Month Milestone

For many people the three-month stage of the relocation is challenging. Sometimes referred to as 'culture shock', it is really a response to the many changes you are adapting to. Knowing this happens can be the first step to both recognising its existence and taking action to change your state. If you have already discovered an effective way of reducing your stress, now is the time to really put it into action.

Keep in mind that stress is a part of life, and one of the challenges of any transition is the loss of existing support systems and how to replace them.

We all make mental comparisons between our home and host cultures, but making judgments encourages us to see one place as 'better' than the other. Try and identify when you use these judgements and the impact it has on your view of what you are describing. Use 'It's not right or wrong – just different' to remind yourself to recalibrate your thinking patterns.

Don't let complacency stop you from journaling. Continuing to observe, reflect and adapt will increase your comfort, confidence and effectiveness.

It's been four months – perhaps it is beginning to feel a little more like home. Re-read your journal to see how your life has evolved. What things are now easy that once were difficult? What are you still working hard to master? Where are your energies being invested most?

Remember why you moved here.

What are your plans and dreams for the next six months? Revisit the Gaining Clarity exercise, and re-evaluate your plans in light of what you have learned about yourself, your new home and your new life.

APPENDIX 1

The Gaining Clarity Exercise

What are your hopes, your plans and your expectations for your new life? We all have them, influencing our behaviours, our adaptation and even our sense of happiness, yet we rarely take the time to put them in words.

Now is the time. Find somewhere peaceful and spend some time putting them on paper. They are probably a combination of many parts of your life, and might be positive (things you are moving towards) or negative (things you are moving away from). Don't worry about finishing it all in one go – you may need a few hours, days or even weeks to capture it all. Just start, and let the rest follow.

More information at: www.expatjournals.com/wheeloflife

APPENDIX 2

Get The Knowledge:
a list of suggested resources for general information.

Geographical information

What do you know about your neighbors? From the bordering countries to the surrounding streets, what does the place that you will call home look like?

There are many wonderful resources to help you start to picture your new home without leaving the comfort of your current one. Look at a map – do you see green spaces or networks of roads?

Google Earth or National Geographic both allow you to not only view the location and landscape, but to zoom in and see neighborhoods, streets and even what the houses look like. Spend some time exploring, so that when you do arrive, it will feel a little more familiar and you will have a better idea of the where to find the things you need or want – parks, shops, or some open space.

http://google.com/earth

http://maps.nationalgeographic.com/maps

Country information

One of the best information sources on countries around the world is the CIA World Factbook. This resource contains a wealth of information about the government, the people, the economy, and the geography. Just glancing at the population information will help you to understand the average local age, how populated areas are, and how old and healthy the people are who live there.

It's useful to compare this to your own home nation to build a better understanding of what those differences might mean. Ask yourself "So what?" For example, lower literacy levels may mean it is more difficult to hire employees or to communicate with people around you unless you speak the local language.

https://www.cia.gov/library/publications/the-world-factbook/index.html

To learn about the history and society of your new home, consider visiting the extensive resources of the Library of Congress. It provides fascinating insights into how past events have shaped the country and its people.

http://lcweb2.loc.gov/frd/cs/list.html

There are many different travel guides available, aimed at everyone from the backpacker on a budget to the luxury traveler. Although you are not a tourist, many of the guides can be very helpful in getting you started, covering everything from how to behave, where to get emergency medical care and useful phrases, to name but a few.

We love *Lonely Planet* guides for the accuracy and breadth of information, the logical layout and their excellent local knowledge, but feel free to choose whatever guide you prefer. Look for one which includes more comprehensive information on the local customs, community and neighborhoods, rather than those that focus exclusively on the short term, hotel based traveler.

The *Lonely Planet* website provides a sample of the style of their guides and some helpful information on aspects such as costs and money, weather, getting around and **health and safety.**

http://www.lonelyplanet.com/places

While you are browsing travel guides, remember to get a **phrasebook** so you can begin to practice some useful phrases. In some places, there are a number of languages and dialects spoken, so double check with the *World Factbook* or with the embassy of that country if you are unsure.

For those of you with a smartphone, there are some great apps available that will make life easier. They serve a range of purposes, so read the reviews carefully to see which will work best for your situation. For an up-to-date list of our favourites, check the http://www.expatjournals.com website.

Culture, society and beliefs and values

There are a number of web based country information resources that can help you to begin to understand the culture and society. Remember a culture is much more than a list of etiquette standards and these may change over time and across social groups. What is acceptable behaviour with one group of people within a country may differ for another.

http://www.countryreports.org

http://www.kwintessential.co.uk/resources/country-profiles.html

If you are interested in learning more about cultural value differences (individualism versus collectivism) take a look at Geert Hofstede's website where you can compare your home and host countries to explore the differences you may encounter.

http://geert-hofstede.com/countries.html

Expat websites and resources

Websites are a great place to find more information and connect with other expats. The ones listed below include country information and blog directories. Also consider searching for other local blogs, Facebook groups and Twitter feeds with information on your host location – often they can be a personal, current and relevant source of knowledge. We have listed some of the more well known sites below, but try a search including the terms 'expat', 'blog' or 'group' and your host location to bring up a wealth of real people sharing their stories.

http://www.expatexplorer.hsbc.com

http://www.internations.org

http://www.talesmag.com

http://www.expatexchange.com

http://www.gatewaylocations.com

http://www.expatwomen.com/expat-women-countries.php

Cost of living data

Having an idea of your cost of living before you arrive is incredibly helpful. There are many resources available – be sure to check a few to get a more accurate comparison. We have included our two favourites to get you started.

http://www.numbeo.com/cost-of-living/

http://www.xpatulator.com

For comparison purposes, the website below lists the US government allowances for employees in different postings.

http://aoprals.state.gov/Web920/location.asp?menu_id=95

Health information

Your local health provider should be your first point of contact for personalised health information that reflects your own medical history. For more general information and guidelines, check your own Foreign Office or the Center for Disease Control and Prevention website.

http://wwwnc.cdc.gov/travel/

Government information about other countries

Our perception of another country is often influenced by our home nation's relationship with that country. Take a moment to find the information from your own government about other countries. Here, for example, are the USA, the Australian Department of Foreign Affairs, the French, the British and the Canadian Foreign Office websites.

http://www.state.gov/misc/list/index.htm

http://www.state.gov/r/pa/ei/bgn/

http://www.dfat.gov.au/geo/

http://www.diplomatie.gouv.fr/en/country-files/

https://www.gov.uk/government/world

http://travel.gc.ca/travelling/advisories

Government travel advice for other countries

In these websites governments provide advice to their citizens travelling abroad regarding the perceived risks of travelling in those countries. Often they include a facility to register as a visitor or sojourner in other countries, so you can receive current information from your home government concerning your host location. Find the website for your home/ passport country and register with them as soon as you arrive.

https://www.gov.uk/foreign-travel-advice

http://smartraveller.gov.au/zw-cgi/view/Advice/

http://travel.state.gov/travel/cis_pa_tw/cis_pa_tw_1168.html

APPENDIX 3

Moving Countdown Checklist

As soon as you make the decision to go:

- Apply for passports.

- Research visas and work permits (for all family members), residency restrictions (for children who will reach adult age while you are there) and schedule applications.

- Research entry and residency requirements for whole family (also pets) including vaccinations.

- Make vaccination appointment schedule and set reminders in your calendar or phone.

- Beg/ borrow/ steal and then READ any resources available on your new location, including age appropriate ones for your children.

- Negotiate relocation package with employer – including a copy of policy for spouse, and ability to request changes as issues arise.

- Review relocation package in detail, including health insurance provision, monetary allowances, shipping allocation, emergency evacuation, early repatriation, dependent care provision, transport to and from host location, etc.

- Make host country contacts and meet informally.

- Begin studying the language and culture of your host country.

- Research living conditions, housing, schooling (including school system and home schooling if necessary), driving requirements and lifestyles.

- Make decision on current housing – sell, rent out, give notice of end of tenancy. Choose professionals to handle sale or property management early.

- Plan an exploratory trip, if possible. Make a list of questions you need answering during the trip.

- Schedule time off for important relocation dates.

4 – 6 Months Before Departure

- Choose moving company and get quotes for removals, shipping and storage. Verify each stage is fully insured.

- Start decluttering the house.

- Inventory possessions, take photographs and arrange insurance.

- Categorize possessions – airfreight/ sea freight/ luggage/ storage/ donate.

- Continue vaccination schedule (family members and pets).

- Make arrangements for pets you will leave behind – allow time to find a home you like for them.

- Schedule medical, dental and eye examinations, and review results. Make any lifestyle changes, treatment plans etc. necessary to maximize health prior to obtaining health insurance. Get direct contact details for current providers.

- Organize important documents, make copies (both photocopies and scanned copies saved to a flash drive, Evernote (www.evernote.com) or Dropbox (www.dropbox.com).

- Make a will and prepare a trust, power of attorney and health care directive/ living will.

- Make arrangements for managing your finances abroad, and understand the cost of your choice.

- Decide what to do with high value or irreplaceable objects (consider a safety deposit box for both these and your important documents – leave the key with a lawyer who you can instruct if necessary).

- Get advice from people in your host country about what personal and household supplies or electronics you might need, and start purchasing. Common items include preferred toiletries, electric toothbrush heads, sun cream, hair color and feminine hygiene. Note that you will need to purchase a multiregion DVD player if you are going to take your DVD collection with you.

3 Months Before Departure

- Schedule routine medical and dental check-ups that would normally fall within the first 3-6 months of arrival, to be completed before you go.

- Request copies of all medical and dental records, check for errors and make digital copies.

- Update the contact details of people you wish to keep in contact with – join a social networking group (e.g. Facebook) for ease of access. Include host country contacts too.

- Transfer as much of your day-to-day bills, banking etc. to online capability.

- Make arrangements for new schools for children and notify your current school of when and where the children will be going. Request copies of school transcripts both for yourself and to be sent to the new school.

2 Months Before Departure

- Buy supplies to be included in household shipment.

- Unlock mobile phone.

- Set up independent email account (e.g. Gmail, Yahoo etc.) and transfer contacts. Notify your email contact list of new address.

- Go through each room of the house and finalise what to take and what to leave. Inventory both categories separately for insurance for shipping or storage.

- Make interim living arrangements (hotel/ short term apartment) for host country.

- Give notice on rental property.

- Check with any host country contacts if they have anything they would like you to bring out for them. Have them send any purchases to your home address.

- Schedule the date for packing up the household contents. Allow at least 3 days before departure.

In The Final Month

- Notify all contractual services (mobile phone, cable/satellite TV, insurance etc.) of date of end of service in writing. Keep copies of all paperwork.

- If you are renting out your home, make list of preferred maintenance/ service engineers and forward to the property management company, along with your contact details. Arrange for the house to be cleaned after your departure.

- Buy a laptop if you don't already own one, and make sure it has Wi-Fi, camera and microphone capability. Learn how to use it. Download Google Hangouts, Skype or other VOIP provider.

- Arrange mail forwarding.

- Finalise new homes for any pets you are not taking with you.

- Notify banks etc. that you will be accessing your accounts from a new location.

- Remind your email contact list of your new address.

- List and collect all important documents and store safely for transport in your hand luggage.

- Pack your luggage before the movers arrive, and store elsewhere to prevent accidental shipping.

APPENDIX 4

Developing Your Cultural Intelligence (CQ)

One of our aims in writing this journal is to help you build your cultural intelligence – your CQ. So what is CQ? It's a practical intelligence that makes the difference between those who adapt well to another cultural environment and those who don't. People with higher CQ are more likely to settle in, work well and live well in a new culture than those with a lower CQ. All good things, for you, in your situation. And most encouragingly, CQ is something which can be developed and increased.

This journal can help you increase each of the four types of CQ described below. How can writing in this journal do that?

CQ Drive: In the journal you will write about your hopes and dreams for your journey. These are the things that will motivate you as you settle in and adapt to the new location. Writing will develop your curiosity about the differences you are encountering – and curiosity is often a source of intrinsic motivation. This motivation is what gives you your energy – or **drive** – as you get up each day and explore and learn about the new culture.

Your observations in stressful situations will help you to develop and strengthen your resilience. Rereading your previous entries will help you to build your confidence and show you your progress.

CQ Knowledge: As you do your research, as you observe and discover new things, you will be building your cultural knowledge. Asking questions through your journal will help you to keep increasing and building on that information. Your notes, your records and information you gain from people you meet will add to your knowledge daily.

CQ Strategy: The core of journaling is you assume the role of an observer of both the world around you and your responses to it. This is the key to CQ Strategy. Your journal will be a place for planning, for reviewing, for noting things to ask your cultural mentor, and for reviewing your own reactions and emotions so you can constantly improve and enhance the way you act within the culture. This is a powerful way to see how those reactions impact on your ability to relate with people and build relationships, and get things done effectively.

CQ Action: As you journal, you take note of the things you do – your **actions**. You will record how successful (or not) you were in different situations. Your journal will also provide an encouraging record of your progress as you improve in language and adapt to local styles of communication or thinking. It will also highlight actions which work best for you, and your use of different communication styles depending on the context.

APPENDIX 5

Essential Documents

One of the most frustrating things about relocating is the paperwork, both the amount required and the amount generated. It's impossible to predict what documents you will need and when, but we have put together a checklist of the most commonly required ones for establishing a new life overseas, and protecting yourself if something goes wrong.

We advise you to make copies of all the relevant documents, store the originals somewhere safe and upload digital copies to secure cloud storage or a portable hard drive. We also recommend you notify a trusted friend, family member or lawyer where the copies can be found in an emergency.

Identity Documents

- Passports (valid for at least 6 months)
- Visas
- Birth certificates
- Marriage certificate/s
- Divorce documentation
- Child custody documentation
- Spare passport photos x 8 each (home and host location sizes)

Estate Planning

- Contacts – friends, family, legal and professional services
- Will
- Trust
- Living Will/ Advance Directive of Health Care
- Summary of Estate
- Life insurance

Financial

- Employer or government issued evidence of annual salary for past two years (e.g. W2 in the USA, P60 in the UK, PAYG Payment Summary in Australia.)
- Most recent pay slips, covering at least two months and evidence of year to date earnings
- Most recent bank statements, covering at least two months, including all pages
- Most recent statements for any other income sources, covering at least two months
- Existing mortgage payment statement
- Social Security card/ number
- Credit cards
- Loan documents

Health

- Health records
- Vaccination records (especially for children)
- Health insurance details
- National Insurance/ Medicare cards (UK/ USA and Australia)

Home

- Contact details – property maintenance and management
- Home title
- Home insurance policy
- Home inventory
- Renter agreement

Education

- School transcript/ evidence of level of study achieved
- Contact details for school and last teacher
- Exam certificates

Career and Employment

- Relocation package/ policy
- Academic certificates
- Professional qualification certificates
- Resumes/ curriculum vitae
- Contact details for references

APPENDIX 6

'In Case Of Emergency' Plan

Trisha and I live at opposite ends of the world, in countries with excellent infrastructure and medical care. Yet over the last few months, both of us have needed to think about our own 'In Case of Emergency' plans.

No matter where you are, you need to have a number of things in place if disaster strikes, whether natural or man-made. You will need to plan for your immediate safety and security, your ability to survive until help arrives, and the resources you will need to get your life back on track as quickly as possible.

Individual requirements will vary according to location and type of emergency, but as a rule, we are aiming for you to get out, get together, stay warm, fed and hydrated and have the necessary information to get back to normal as quickly as possible. It takes a little preparation, but once in place, is straightforward to update. So in order of priority, here's your emergency checklist.

Getting Prepared

Know where your documents are, and have scanned, digital copies saved to a portable hard drive or a secure cloud storage service.

Make regular backups of your computer and all your photos.

Have a household emergency kit that contains, at the very minimum:

- 3 days water supply (1 gallon water per person, per day)

- 3 days non-perishable food and can opener
- Battery powered/ wind up radio
- Wind up flashlight
- First Aid kit
- Whistle
- Shelter (tarpaulin/ plastic sheeting and duct tape/ lightweight tent)
- Moist towelettes

In addition, add three days supply of any family specific requirements – infant formula, diapers, moist wipes, pet food etc.

Getting Out

Have an exit plan in place that includes:

- Safe exit routes, that you have practised as a family
- Clear family roles – who grabs the bags, the pets, the children etc.
- A destination – the family car, a neighbors home, a landmark

Getting Together

Emergencies don't always happen when you are all in the same place, so plan:

- **Meet up point:** Local library, landmark etc. Choose somewhere where you will be able to find each other easily, and make sure your children are able to communicate the meetup point to any adult. Check with children's schools to find out their meetup points and evacuation protocols.

- **Communication:** Have a central point of contact for all family members to use, preferably someone out of the area/ country. Use text messages for most efficient communication, VOIP's such as Skype, Rebtel and Viber often work when regular cell phone service is overloaded. Keep a written copy of emergency information with each family member in case you lose your cell phones/ battery power/ medical emergency.

Stay Warm

Each family member should have an **individual backpack** they are able to carry themselves, which should contain:

- Change of clothes appropriate to the climate/ local conditions, with spare underwear and socks.
- Warm/ waterproof coat
- Comfortable, strong shoes or sneakers
- Energy bars
- Water bottle and purification tablets/ water filtration system
- Prescription medications
- Sleeping Bag
- Wind up torch
- Card games/ toys/ paper and crayons

In addition, the adult backpack should have waterproof bags containing:

- Personal identity documents (passports, visas, driving licences etc.)
- Home, medical and life insurance details
- Original documents that are difficult to replace (e.g. birth and marriage certificates etc.)
- Portable hard drive with scanned copies of photos, essential documents, computer backups

- Cash
- First Aid kit and instructions

Where appropriate:
Infant formula and supplies, diapers, wipes, dry pet food (3 day supply), feminine care supplies.

But Wait There's More...

We want to give you more. More information, resources, and exercises to work through and write about. We want to provide resources for those of you who are helping others on their expat journey.

But we want **this** book to be a diary. One written by you and telling your story. We want what you have in your hands to be **all about you**.

So we have created a website which includes extended versions of many of the exercises and resources, and where you can find many more tips and suggestions to making expat life the adventure and experience you imagined when you first thought about embarking on this journey. You can read about the research, which provides the evidence base for our work in this book, and discover other professionals who have written extensively about their own work and experiences and can provide valuable insight into yours.

There are also many additional resources too personal to be included in this book, which will be invaluable in keeping your expat life organised and giving you room to focus on the social and emotional process of Finding Home Abroad.

And finally, we have included the gift of community – a list of authors who have written both from a personal and professional perspective, who can inform, inspire and encourage you as you chart your own unique course.

But SHHH.... the website is just for you, as a benefit and bonus for buying the book. We ask that you don't share the link, but rather encourage those who might find our work useful to discover the whole package for themselves. We look forward to seeing you over at
www.expatjournals.com/FHAgetmore571

About The Authors

Trisha Carter is an organisational psychologist, renowned cultural intelligence specialist and founder of www.cicollective.com, a comprehensive online resource that supports successful cross-cultural adaptation. An expat herself, she has over 15 years experience as an intercultural coach and trainer, helping hundreds of individuals and families to transition successfully. When not presenting at international conferences or delivering training to government and corporate organisations, she can be found at home in Sydney, Australia.

Rachel Yates is a writer, speaker and creator of www.ExpatLifeLine.com. She combines her personal and professional experience to deliver online resources for relocating individuals and families, blending advice, support and effective planning strategies to empower, inform and inspire. When not serving on the Board of Directors for Families in Global Transition, or hiking with her dogs, she can be found in San Francisco, USA.